Flight Path

Cynthia Neely's poems in *Flight Path* (Aldrich Prize Honorable Mention, 2013) embrace the world of birds from gray jay and loon to raven and wren, encompass leave-taking flights both human and animal, perceive the poem as a creature taking flight, and merge child with nestling. Here are winged departures, lives flown, a mind with sense flown, lives diminished by cancer, hands of illness as "brown speckled birds," a son leaving the nest, and the lost, unborn child who flew away, sacrificed to cancer. I recommend this book with its graceful narrator who grieves what's flown and yet delights to sing in the midst of wilderness and wings.

--- Marly Youmans, 2013 Aldrich Prize judge

Flight Path

Cynthia Neely

*To Hillary
in friendship
& appreciation
Forest Grove 2014
Cynthia*

Aldrich Press

ISBN 13: 978-0692215845

Cover Art: *When the Bough is Broken* 2013, © Cynthia Neely

Kelsay Books
Aldrich Press
24600 Mountain Avenue 35
Hemet, California 92544

Contents

For Tom –
always the music
in my life

Flight Path

Each thud sends me running
out the sliding-glass doors
to find them, some already dead,

necks broken, some curled-feet
in the air, bodies twitching
like aspen leaves, one last shiver

before the wind dies down.
Varied thrush, nuthatch,
ruby-crowned kinglet--

glassy eyed but still
breathing. I pick them up,
tiny hearts beating

hard in the cup of my palms.
Some struggle, then settle, give in.
Is this what it means to hold life

in your hands? Who would not
want to stroke each flight-feather,
study each eye-stripe, wing-bar?

Finger each bill, fine as pencil lead,
enter each black bead of eye, blinking,
blinking, closing.

Our Scars

The long line along my spine,
the new ligament in your knee,
the gash the chainsaw slashed

as you ordered our unruly woods, a wound
so deep you could see right down
to the blanched heart of it. So pristine it didn't bleed.

The slice above my breast to take the snake
of tubing to my own rebellious heart, a portal for all things
chemical and mean to clean the cancer from my cells.

And that deep seam from pubis to navel
like the cleft of an over-ripe peach,
muscles un-repaired in the haste of need,

the speed of my life gathered in, now
a reminder, each mirror glance, of that chance,
that child, unborn.

The love-tap from a bobcat on your chin,
a boy's first lesson about all things wild
that can't be tamed.

My Father Took Each Dying Bird

gape-billed, dull-eyed,
from the shoebox where I'd
placed it, nested in a pile

of wilting grass and torn tissue
soiled with blood-tinged excrement.
He carried them

and his red-handled shovel
out to the lot beside
the tadpole-hunting puddle

where honeysuckle hung low
over moldy mattresses and half-
buried bike wheels, spokes

broken. I found my birds
injured or pushed too soon from nests
and believed eye-droppers of sugar-water

could make them well
and then they'd stay with me,
something wild and winged.

I never followed, never knew how much
each act of mercy hurt, never saw him
wipe the shovel's blade in the dirt.

A Quieter Place in the World

after a line from Stephen Dunn

The year I finally got a horse and rode the air
of the East Cascades, tasted the acrid pine
in the ponderosa stands, I understood

I had waited too long,
had become a creature of what's easy
and disconnected among the familiar,

scarfed and buttoned-up.
But this muscle of gallop, this horse, oh
he worried and excited me, brought me

a new vocabulary: cantle, bridle, girth,
the dearth of my understanding
immeasurable. After the sun

had warmed the earth
and hay had swelled his belly,
I'd saddle him up and lead him to a rock,

a makeshift mounting-block,
talk gentleness till he'd bend,
signal me to climb on.

Walk on. Show me
the stump that could be a bear
or that tawny mound

that looks like a mountain lion
crouched low. I didn't know
how much world there was to worry about:

that stout heft of grass,
that waggle of wind-ruffed brush.
I trained my eye to see like a horse.

To be like a horse
is to be something hunted.
He forgave me who I was.

In the evenings, after feedings
he would ask me to teach him
my language. Back, over, step,

on-by. He was a faster learner than I.
When winter came, and the winds
drifted snow into furrows he stopped

eating and went down. When his eye
dulled, I kept my promise, then
took a quieter place in the world.

Thick

The scent comes first, almost
fresh, like spring soil,
although it's the end
of September.

Ravens, already busy
with the cleanup: liver,
stomach, heart – large
as a man's, still warm, flaccid.

Hunters had bled
and gutted the bear at the edge
of the river, on a sandy lip
where all they'd had to do was wait,

near the fruit-laden elderberry,
its branches bent and broken
by the forager's weight,
berry-clusters now dangling

near the river's surface,
deep red-purple. Blood
still pools on the pebbled floor
despite the current.

Birding at the Potholes

Red epaulets flash on marsh grass,
draw our scopes from familiar fields
of view, the hunt for something
to lift us. We search

for cranes, whose stilt legs barely
carry them, whose wings loft them
graceless – a run, stumble, flap – before air
becomes a substance that will bear them.

Our son follows, crane-legged, iPod-eared.
He doesn't hear the calls that pull us forward,
doesn't see the meadowlark, bibbed and shining,
the porcelain painted puff of chucking quail.

His footprints are as big as ours, but
he won't fill them, his head bowed, back bent
to minutiae: ants, scat, a feathered sign of struggle,
the treasure of pebble and spent shotgun shell.

He has no interest in our quest – the present
and the past are all right there
under his feet, no need to scan the sky
for cranes, already gone.

Shepherds

What's happened to the herring gulls,
that ubiquitous bicker? Where are the many
who'd scream and wheel above our island picnics,

faces tilted, cocked-eye to the blueberry pie
on the smooth rock below?
Now in their place, double-crested cormorants,

and their attendant gathering of terns
that twist and twitter in a hunger flash, cacophonous
confetti-cloud, fork-tailed and mean-mouthed,

snatching minnows scared up
by the surging tide of cormorants,
this flock they shepherd.

Seven big boats in the bay today – still
the loons protect their nest, hoot and flap:
over here! over here!   I can't help them.

Or the gulls. Or my son who is fledged and flexing
his own hollow-shafted wings, trying
to divide and divine the answer from its promise.

I no longer take the first burning bite
from the silver-handled spoon. No need,
too-late, to stroke his back, clear a path

through the detritus of his room, books
and ancient underwear, damp towels on the floor,
Lego long forgotten in a drawer.

I cradle a baby swallow flung from his neat nest,
spindle-necked and patch of downy crown,
sallow fat along his twig-fine breastbone.

Shad-flies I stuff
down that absurdly open throat
hold him here for only a moment.

An Accident of Hope

The worst of anyone can be, finally,
an accident of hope
  — Anne Sexton

Water slaps the sides of the tinner
tethered to the summer dock
at the edge of the bay. The end of the day.

My son is sighing in his loft.
Not satisfied sighs, more like he wants
to escape something that follows him,

that just won't let him be,
that hollows him. What is it we can't see?
What foolishness our hope's become,

a Cracker Jack-boxed plastic treasure,
awaited prize that is our son? Some crumb
of sweetness only hope can measure?

I've watched the boy dive deep in the bay,
remembering how he'd kicked and swam in me.
The cicada had already shed its skin,

buzzed its tuneless song among the branches,
a hollowed shell abandoned on the wing
before I finally got a chance to hold him.

This afternoon he laughed his man-laugh
playing cards with cousins at the long table,
showing them his better face, the half

that says he's happy. Then he broke
into song, the bass part for which there is
no tune, as the whitethroat sang of Canada

in the arthritic pine, knuckled over
on the northern shore. We say *this will pass,*
though it never does, we say *it will all be fine.*

Nadeau Island, Georgian Bay, Summer 2012

The International Joint Committee settles
on a do-nothing policy regarding the escalating
loss of water through the St. Clair River locks.

I woke to a shroud draped over the bay
as if the water itself was on fire. A fog
with not a drop of the familiar

moisture that curls my hair, the pages
of my book. Not water vapor, but particulates
unparticular about where they blew. North

of here is burning – but not this island –
Leviathan granite, whales' backs
barnacled with thousand year old lichens:

viridian, turquoise, cadmium-orange.
A painter's spattered palette.
This rock, marked and pocked,

the glacier's careless calligraphy unchanged
for ten-thousand years. And now the bay
is emptying, water levels dropping

each year, like some huge hand
scoops it out, leaving the high-water mark,
a bathtub ring.

A vast mouth opened
so ships could navigate once-narrow throats.
It swallows lakes Huron and Michigan.

One-hundred million gallons an hour.

But this island will remain,
a steeper one on quieter water.
The loons will leave,

the inland pond dissipate, its scum
shrivel like lifeless frog-skin,
the back cove will flatten

to mud and jetsam, Javex bottles, boat-
bumpers, the remains of ancient docks,
the fish no longer spawning there.

The fragrant water lilies' waxy
petals and shining pads, the scarlet
cardinal flower. Gone.

The west wind that bent these pines
to bonsai will sweep over more land,
less water – bring heat instead of cool.

And we with our tools, our ancient quest
for fire, the land blazing and all that
fresh water disappearing. Like us,

water seeks the path of least resistance,
a dredge of deepening channel
running to the sea.

Rattler

At dusk we call the dog who doesn't come,
find she's cornered a snake under the deck,
her furious tail a give-away.

Last night, a big fight and the bite of silence
between us. Oh, we built our silence up,
brick and mortared it. Such important work!

Almost an entire day, the sheer toil of it.

Now this snake, thick, gravid, its tail
as delicate as our boy's first baby bracelet.
We pull the dog away, together bend close,

examine the patterned scales,
such perfect camouflage,
that unhurried, unblinking stare.

Like That

We wore plaid skirts, pleats
like knives, and white
button-down shirts with loops
on the back, loafers, tarnished
with copper pennies, scuffed
home from school the back way, down
over the dike, ducking by the creek
with a pack of Tareytons
from Sherry's mother's purse.

We practiced French inhaling,
pulling the acrid smoke
from our mouths in twin-tailed
wisps into flared nostrils,
eyes welling. We whispered,
wondered who would
be the first to allow some boy
to probe our smoky mouths
with his alien tongue.

We named our-kids-to-be,
two or three each, though later
Sherry would decide against children,
I would lose my unborn,
and none of us were still friends

by the time Debby had a steady
with a car, cut class
to drive the back roads fast
and far, left school for good
with a fat squall of a baby.

But back then, on weekends
we'd walk to town, to the five-and-dime,
order cherry Cokes with real cherries
and extra fizz, spritz Brut
on our wrists from trial bottles
and dream about boys
who'd smell like that.

Whatever

after reading Tony Hoagland's "Space Program"

In the history of American music, I was born
between the Boogie Woogie Bugle Boy and The Beat
of a Different Drum.

I ducked under desks, dodged bombs and balls,
fancied the quiet types who had something
to say.

Conceived in the womb of keen,
I grew up in the world
of cool. School still meant an education

for boys, an avocation for girls, a dive in the pool
of typists, minimum wage for a page
fingered-out fast, our single chance

to figure out fast how to someday land
the boss. Then the movement swung
to the freed breasts of liberation,

turning on, tuning out, making love
not war.

He was born between Smells Like
Teen Spirit and Toxic, into Ninja Turtles
and talking teapots, weaned on Tree Top,

from the bound breast of free-love's failure
and just say no, grew into the world
of whatever, totally. The last time I spoke to him

his ears were budded and busy, his battles
not under desks but displayed on them. As usual
I tried to explain it to him,

about life, the world as I know it,
his fingers faster than mine
had ever been, turned off,

tuned in, already knowing more
than I had ever known.

Parenthood

We take
what we can get

and then wonder how
he got here, wild root

of hair shocking
his forehead. Jesus,

we hadn't figured
on this, these answered

prayers. *O* we say
O My. Where

did he come from, so
unlike me, you, the two

of us frivolous, he steadfast,
unbending, serious

bent to his books.
He doesn't look

like either of us either.
A rare bird, not

of our feather. But
whether we want to

or not, we are besotted
by this nestling

sprawling so comfortably
in this tree of ours

even as he takes off
running in his size twelve

and a halfs. Halfway leaving,
halfway staying behind.

A Distant V

Unwelcome as the gulls they join,
those hunched old men with necks drawn in
to dirty gray overcoats, convened
as if for pinochle
or gin,

the Canada geese arrive,
honking into town like tourists,
or masked, black-caped gypsies,
caravans arranged in rows
of stubbled corn.

But I love these denizens of dumps
and fallow fields who wed
for life and raise their young
in unison, until their brood
leaves home for good.

By tomorrow's dawn they'll be gone,
a distant V, a lonely lack of sound.

Love is a Wilderness

We were an island in the bay, the days
like palindromes. Dark before light.
Moon before sun. Long ago,

in the wilds, in the tent we made
of our bed, we found a peace, tenuous
and tenacious as a spider's web,

in a place as hard as heartwood,
burl and bark, dense as ironwood. Love
was a wilderness – twisted stalk

and Solomon's seal, lady's slipper
and slippery elm, anarchy
of woodland and weeds.

We were those branches
and grasses bent to the breeze,
accessories to the draw and pull.

Lately my back's been turned, a fence
of flannel and down. But last night
I let you raise my nightgown

past each slack arm and over my head,
like I was the girl whose skin might still
lie faultless, under your hands, against your lips.

Undone

Beads slowly roll, fall
from the tumbler, the cracked cubes
prismatic in the afternoon sun.

And I'm motionless, the glass
to my lips, mid-sip.

Minnows waltz about my feet
in careful choreography
and I wait.

Waiting is what I'm good at.

I imagine myself the mink, or that I'm
Great and Blue and patient and true and you
will come to me.

Come to me.

Let me show you all I know:
how the skin shines with a touch
and spittle glistens on a lip,
how fingers form a perfect fit
in the hollow of a back,
when night eclipses noon.

Come to me.

Make me believe
the loon has cried for me,

forlorn, dark form.
I'm undone by the sun.
I wait.

Come.

You Can Close Your Eyes

When I first watched your fingers form
the chords to *Fire and Rain*, your head bent

in prayer to the song, I saw you
like some Messiah, like James himself,

long-haired and blue-jeaned,
and the music rushed my veins

like tripping in the backseat
of a borrowed station-wagon,

going to Carolina, if only in our minds.
Was it so long ago when our lungs were filled

with longing? Now the cloth we wove
is threadbare, shining, worn as the fabric

of that Buick's bench seat, aged
as the scarred body of the Gibson,

slack necked, strummed to decrepitude,
fatally out of tune, leaning on the wall

behind the couch, trying to catch its breath
or remember the words.

Birdland

"In the split second of eternity, what do we know
that isn't before speaking?" — James Grabill

Near the end of his life, Charlie Parker
had nowhere to go so he rode the subway

to the end, then rode it back again.
He stood in front of Birdland in the rain

with nothing left to say. Music plays
inside our home, in a mellow tone, Black Cat

purrs a wheezy tune, cockatiels whistle and buzz;
my husband's hands clasp ebony, mahogany,

feather nylon strings. His fingers move
of their own accord, an articulated chord,

careful to convey what he's unable to say, while outside,
a red-tailed hawk completes a fence post in the rain.

Winter Songs

Every winter morning she flutters –
flitting, head cocked, peering
into each window — inspects

each junction of beam that joins
this home. At dawn I hear her
prodding, her slender, slightly

down-turned bill, probing for a gap
large enough to let her in.
Sweeeeet?? she asks, like the song

inside me seeking to get out. Plumage
plumped soft in the still frigid air, white
throat expansive, the canyon wren

thrums a tune, as I hear my husband
downstairs, fingers bending nylon
into notes of rosewood and spruce.

Coffee brews and wafts
between the chords, suspended,
like sevenths, in the air.

Gone Like Ghosts

Day three on the Dempster,
the land before us opens, wide
and wild, and lichen-lined.

We scan the taiga. My camera
clicks – clicks again – stutters. Futile.
A raven laughs.

And you say this: *Come back in April.*
Then you will see the caribou. Drive
the ice-road to Tuktoyaktuk.

Your face, ancient as the tundra, trails
of a million hooves etched there, is tanned
as the land for which your Gwich'in are named.

Your great-granddaughter grins,
shows us the marten's pelt, the mink,
the fur-lined caribou-hide hut,

tells us she's never seen a wolf,
though her cousins have – three
ran right in front of them

at winter hunting grounds,
gone like ghosts, before
she looked to see.

You smile a gap-toothed smile,
jingle the loonies in your pocket,
politely wait for us to go.

Inside Passage – Prince William Sound

Twelve-thousand years passed by
in the blink of leviathan's eye.
Rivers of Pleistocene ice

still gouge and grind through rock and rime,
leaving in their wake a place where time gone
is not regretted.

Here, Pinks pirouette, seemingly happily,
on the way to their conclusion.
They practice

their leap of life, before
they are devoured by the mouths
of rivers and streams that draw them in,

even against the flow. Silvers break,
slice the surface in tandem, ripples rise,
are swallowed, rise again.

If I would look with eyes not dimmed
by dreams or desires, by foolishness or fears,
could I unearth an instant, within a blink,

that's as clean as a breaching breath,
flukes saluting, slapping in unison,
before returning to the sea?

Crossings

I

My grandmother crosses on a ship
from England, her books and purse tight
in her lap. A spinster at thirty, to find a mate,
she leaves a lush life of birding and golf,

a botanist grandfather for whom orchids
are named, and a mother disappointed
by a daughter who prefers hiking, walking
stick in hand, to serving suitors tea.

Crossing the waves of chance and change,
Grandfather too boards a boat – from Ireland,
from famine, from fear and unrest,
an Orangeman's boy, a farmer – he plows his way

through sea and soil, to the interior of Canada,
to a room in the boarding house
where proper paths cross, briefly, barely,
and they embark on their affair

of letters and of words, over time, over
distance, he adrift on prairies of grain, she
held tight in the lap of polite society,
thousands of miles apart.

II

I trace the map
of courteous correspondence,
its solemn, slow crossing to each in turn,
describing day-to-day happenings, ardor,

infatuations long since whispered, long unfelt.
And because she is no longer young
and he is the only man to ask, she agrees,
after years of posted passion, to marry him.

She travels by train – for days, sitting up –
her wedding cake upon her broad lap, her thick
knees unable to meet, wheels clacking
resolute and forward toward life

with a man to whom she has hardly spoken
a living word, to a role she is ill prepared to fill:
a grain inspector's wife, a confidante
of secrets she does not want and refuses to know.

III

Grandmother tells me how grand
her life will be, after Grandfather dies,
something he has alternately threatened
and promised for years. She will live

on Vancouver Island and have a garden again.
She was there once, the garden attendant
politely amazed by her knowledge
of each Latin name, as he wheeled her

large chair-ridden frame, blanket over her knees,
through the exhibits, one by one. She pictures herself
on the ferry once again, her bird books in her lap,
spanning the sound to the life she was meant to have.

Grandmother's crossing came too soon
for her to live her garden-island dream.
I picture her passing, a smile on her lips, launched
on another broad voyage, once more on her own.

I have her tip-top table, her beloved books of birds,
and the painting of hydrangea, its looping Latin name
inscribed along with mine on the back.

IV

I still see her as I saw her
when I was a child - before Parkinson's,
before disease took what freedom she had.
I glimpse her, scarfed against the cold,

wrapped in an old fur coat that had crossed
with her from England, with the hand-carved
tip-top table, the scarred sea-chest with her trousseau:
china and silver and the fine family name.

She walks to get the mail, crossing
the whitewashed lane bordered with snow
and wagon-wheels. She has treats
in her fur-lined pockets, sunflower seeds

pursed in her lips, and chickadees landing
on her shoulders and on her head.

Passing

Passing the 76 on the way
to Costco, you get the urge
to just keep going, straight
past and up through

the desert plateau, its crooked
basalt cliffs, uprooted orchards,
their poplar windbreaks
ragged, sagging

their branches beseeching,
water long withheld. Well past
the Come Ons, the Welcomes
and the Dewdrop Inns,

past sinking porches
with peeling paint,
the rusted out Miley
and the lone and lonely

tail-swish roan, past the single-
wides, the duallys, the triple-bay
repair shops; past the makeshift
memorial – monument to someone

who tried to pass but should have waited
along the miles and miles of fallow fields
with fences holding nothing.

Waiting

I know what Proust knew: an odor,
even a pleasant one like peppermint, can kindle
responses unbidden. But I don't sense
any odor at all, and sparrows

still flit outside the window, the clouds
still scud across the sun. My hair still swings
along my spine. But nausea nudges my throat again
the moment we enter and the receptionist asks

*Do you have a port-a-cath dear?*to a woman waiting
beside us who chirps, Yes!   *Are you ready then?*
Of course!   as if she waits to be seated in candlelight
with a dinner date. My husband is here

for tests – to tell us if his esophagus
is normal or not, with all that *not* implies:
Will I hold his hand as he'd held mine; clutch
the pan to catch his fear; shave his head

just as he'd sheared memories smooth; wait
for that thing with feathers? In the waiting room,
I watch them all with the familiarity of a sister
and want to take their hands, that flutter

like brown speckled birds, into mine and kiss them quiet,
though it's been twenty years since I belonged
to this odd fellowship of blood and tubes,
the curative cocktails of poison and pain, collapsed veins,

where our kerchiefed heads and browless eyes unveiled
stories no one but us would want to know. And here
I am again, as if I'd never gone –
home, whole, healed, back to a tidy life.

Here they are again, the same sallow faces, cheerful
in the pattern of routine, the truth of it
sharper than a scalpel, something to count on.

Untying the Knot – *for Camille*

It's hard to sleep, you told me, next to a man
who's dying. And I could imagine

you lying stiff, unmoving, unwilling
to know, afraid to close your eyes

and miss his passing, but wanting
to untie the knot, the coiled dread,

the snake in your chest. For a month
he has had nothing to sustain him

but patience: yours, family's, friends',
who watch his belly balloon

with the tumors that feed there
while his limbs wither. Weeds.

The last time I saw John, he was halfway
gone to another place, folded in

on himself, eyes far away, a palm upturned
as if in supplication. I held his hand, still

beautiful and large. He did not squeeze mine
in return, did not answer my whispered plea,

though his lips parted as if ready to speak.
He might have known when I was there

or when I'd gone, though I pray he didn't
understand that sometimes I visited

not just for him but so I could feel
the lump of panic rise and know that I'm alive.

And This Remains

I heard your mother found you
in your bed, as if asleep,
your affairs all tidy, neat,
the glass sat in the sink, clothing
folded at your feet.
And this remains

your mother's final memory of you,
the one she has to keep.
You waited until spring,
thought the timing would be right
and planned it just as carefully
as the way you threaded skis through
tight white-mantled trees.

Why antifreeze, I wonder?
Wouldn't sleeping pills suffice?
As your gut disintegrated,
did you think it might keep ice from
forming in your soul,
a man who so loved winter, only snow
could keep him whole?

I have to think I'm lucky –
my last memory of you
is a swirl of snow in vortex
behind a disappearing back, sweeping
swift down Cowboy Mountain
in the trail of your deep tracks.

Narrow and True

Driving through Browns Junction
we wonder out loud: is it the brown
vastness that named it, or is a David
or a John or a Robert responsible

for joining something here? Train tracks,
roads that meet and diverge and end
...where? At the diner,
Tanya takes the orders

in a brown uniform with a tan apron,
auburn hair pulled back in a thick braid;
only her earrings give a glimpse
of who she might truly be

as she notes our request for eggs
and hashbrowns and thanks us *hon*
back with our coffee, in a *jif,* the creamer
turns it taupe.

Jackson Browne's "Somebody's Baby"
commands the juke box; Tanya's earrings
sparkle and sway. We want to stay
here in this town, where the main streets still run

narrow and true, and the corner bar shares
the brown-bricked building with the Post Office
and the neighbors are happy
with the color of their lives.

Harbor

I wear my yellow boots
to walk the wet edge
where harbor seals calved
and left their stain. It will wash away

(like the red flushed from the bowl,
 disappearing, blushed and muted, concentric)

while gray whales surface,
blow and sigh, sink
and swim.

The Mountain Shrugged

Then, I am thin, but convinced
I am fat. My hair, still long,
your joy, shines

like our summer-colored skin.
You gaze with a fullness
you still hold for me.

Later, when the chemo
takes my hair, my hope, our child,
you are afraid to look, convinced

I am disappearing, fading
like this photograph.

Now, time steals time.
Barely a chance to glance, full,
like then in a photo that does not show

how the shoulder of the mountain shrugged
into her spring shawl of green, shed it then
in fall to favor white, like the veil I wear
to hide my thin skin.

Comfort

The sheets were pristine, so clean. Wait, go back . . .
The air . . . yes. The air was clean
like a baby's breaching breath . . . no
wait. Back further.

Before my pen described a needle.

Still, before a needle stilled
your life. And Mother needed
not to cradle me
like an infant, or beg me

to remember floating on the bay.
Before the needle did its seeking
through belly swell and amniotic sea.

Stop   wait   further

Before your father shaved my head
Before the wigs I didn't like
Before I shopped for scarves instead

No No No. Before
                the drip drip drip

the cysplat-poisoned veins
discreetly positioned pans
the vague white-coated comfort:
You can always have another...

Before the errant cell
Before I had to tell
I'd choose

me
over you.

Yes, further, further. Before

before, when the air was clean,
when I was clean, and wings were filled,
and you still floated on your own private bay.

Before I balanced on reflection's edge,
lay quiet on pristine sheets with stirrupped feet.

Before I harbored sparrows in my breast
and could not speak
for fear of losing those that fluttered darkly
to escape.

Climacteric

You woke today to an ache
you thought was spent – that season
already mourned and set aside,
flushed away like pink-tinged tissue.

It's a late-March-snow in February, far
too early to be so transient; yet
its whitewash is not unwelcome to the grime
of the fading season. Even now,

as wasps stumble out of the woodwork, fumble
drunken and useless on gray stone floors, winter
begins its end, always before you are ready, always
before your mind has softened

to the idea of it. You hold on too long,
as if letting go will lose…what?
The clean and cold, the muffled
and muffed, safely layered in wool and white?

Or the weightlessness that comes with snow?
It's not that you dread the beginning
of the new, but the ending
of the old. Still you lighten your step

when the earth is young, green rising,
and despair spring petals' fade.
You bask in the heat of long days,
relish the taste of salt, then miss the sweat of it

in coming shadows. And oh how
you whistle so you can see your breath
in the first frost of fall, but grieve
that last leaf's bright tumble.

Broken Water

Sometimes I allow myself
to wonder how our lives might be
had time not turned and left us, broken
water in its wake. Your face would grace
our Christmas cards, your exploits
bragged to all.

Sometimes I can hear you
berating your brother as he bends
to his books, about his mathematical mind,
his lack of interest in his looks, chiding him
for his childishness, grinning
about the girls who wait for him
to finally figure it out.

Sometimes I can see you
as I think you might have been.
Your skin would trap the summer,
long limbs draped out to dry
on our granite island, solid,
smooth and warm with radiant heat.
Your eyes would be the color of mine.

But most times I can only
see you as you were,
alone, adrift on private seas.
You surface and then dive again, lost,
even as you breach and turn.

Sometimes I can see you
swimming in the bay.
Your strong strokes
break the water.

Stones In Our Pockets

Up the Chiwawa River we find the best stones:
granite, schist, quartzite, smoothed
by time and waiting.

All have different hefts but still they fly.
Air holds them, as if the letting go would lose them,
like children already grown, or never born.

One small stone is shot with white,
another bright with golden flecks like those
that might have lit your eyes as they light mine.

And this one looks like glitter-skin
of salmon that brushed past it. They shimmer
when wetted: jewels, too precious now to use

or leave behind, abandoned like caddisfly homes,
glued hovels at the wet edge of darkness. We linger
long, my son and I, still searching for that perfect rock,

the one that can satisfy a skipper of strange stones
that skitter across the surface
like Goldeneyes landing.

I've Heard Twelve Thousand Bees

Perhaps it was the lateness of the hour
or the tepid taste of metal in my mouth
like tungsten on my tongue, or that flower,
deep vermillion, in the field behind the house.
Like a million grains of sand, mica
sifting as if shoveled into air –
it's the passing of the day – it's like a
dusty moth or a dusky backlit pair
of sparrows past the corner of my eye.
What is it I'm reminded of? A lie

can lie between you. It's been said,
again, again, a mantra, or a chime
you have to give it time. Now how we dread
each end of day, finality of line.
Is it the word *goodbye* we see, were shown
that thousand times? I've heard twelve thousand bees
can rise and move as one, to shift a throne
of honeycomb and follow just one queen.
I rise, I rise, I muscle my veined wings
but none will follow. None are gathering.

In My Next Life I Might be a Moth

A mottled moth seeks my wine,
hatched from birdseed

and we can't rid our home
of them. Their cocoons

line the line where ceiling
meets wall, tenacious sacks

that won't be moved,
can't be pried free

by those who think
themselves in charge

of this planet of arthropods,
these millers fluttering

every evening, looking
for a drink in which to drown.

Wild

For several years we watched him
prowl our mountainside, puffed and proud,
a slight gimp to his gait but a track
that traveled straight,

footprints single-filed in snow.
Amber eyes stared back at us
when we would meet, our wooded paths
crossing closer with each reunion.

His ruff, in auburn shadow, formed
a perfect frame for his face, a coat
any Inuit would envy, guard hairs stiff
and fringed with frost.

Last week, we spied him with a mate
cavorting on the county road,
moving off just far enough
each morning when we'd pass,

a bow to her curtsey, a breath
of vapor to pricked ear, a choice
to chase or be chased, a glimpse of gray
and sable on a purple dappled stage.

We found him late this morning
his coyote pelt still plush
but stiff and fringed with frost,
a small red hole – the ravens will eat today.

Cocooned

The fog is in. We button our coats
against the dank. And what we don't know

rises and parts, sets in again. Frost
would have us choose a road, mend a wall.

But we'd work too hard at it, digging up
old poems, pick and shovel, body

and soul, trombones moaning
like Mardi Gras on Basin Street,

instead of here, where we sit tonight
beneath these wind-crippled pines, no road,

no wall in sight; instead, we tend
our wine, sip our liquor, lick our wounds,

like salted margaritas, limed green
as luna moths whose caterpillars soon

will spin cocoons, while days diminish,
nights lengthen, cryptic as those years.

Could it be a mistake? What difference
would one road make?

This Poem

for Kwame Dawes

This poem arrives as a promise,
broken. It comes in winsome words

without the truth to back it up, hands
stuffed deep in its empty pockets.

It slouches in its easy chair. Silly poem,
beseeching us to trust it, teaching us

that a poem is not a lesson. This poem
has no beginning but it wants to end

as a story of love . . . or death.
It doesn't know, its final message carved

from the extremes of caring
too little or too much.

A Day Like Any Other

I scan my bills, toss junk while sorting mail,
then set the table, stir and taste my tea,
still waiting for the phone to ring, the stale
dull breath of morning wakening. "The sea
is starting to recede. A record tide..."
reception sputters "...101.1".
I pick a scab of candle wax. Outside
the paling moon is soon to be outdone,
the way it often seems when light's dispersed
and sun's just up but not quite taken hold,
like eighteen years ago today, when first
you grew in me, before I could be told
you'd raise the tides, a moon in perigee,
but you would wane, so far, so far, from me.

Inheritance

after The Hare With the Amber Eyes
by Edmund de Waal

Eighty-four and slightly stooped
still impeccable in herringbone
he'd carry them from the cabinet
hand them to you one by one

the hare with the amber eyes
the samurai in his helmet
the tiger turned to snarl

You'd tumble them in your hands
search by feel where signatures hid

sole of a sandal
hornet's thorax
tail of a rat wrapped
round a fish

He'd let you return them to their case
and fill the little cups with water
so the ivory wouldn't split

Living the longest is hard, he said
and your eyes did not meet

October's tree outside the window
covered in goldfinches
still blazed gold
after the finches had flown

Trick or Treat

When you were two
you laughed a laugh

like a man's, deep
and full, containing nothing

but pure pleasure. Strangers
on a bus once laughed

with you, kept on chuckling
right out the door.

Now your smile
is stone-ciphered.

Mineral.
A man's set of jaw.

Fourteen years ago
you navigated the neighborhood

alone in a Skywalker cape
back when it seemed

we each were waiting
on our tip-toes

for all the goodness we should receive,
opening the bag to have it filled up.

Who knew then
the sack of disappointments?

That heavy satchel
lugged home each day,

unopened. A boy alone
on his trundle bed.

It Takes a Certain Sort of Sanity

to sit in Dostoevsky's steamy kitchen
upon a noisy waking
the char of yesterday still smoking
a hint of sulfur in the air

no pleasure
no daydreams

no pencil no pen
no horse to ride
the poor thing rendered

no mercy
no pity

a copy of the news sits on the kitchen table
a sparrow broken-necked below the window's pane

When the Bough is Broken

In the parking lot of a fast food joint,
a juvenile crow falls from its roost.
Pin-feathered pain. Raucous adults surround it,
cacophonous cannibals, picking and plucking.
Its mother, head thrown back, a trumpet of anguish,
wings outstretched to shield it, finally folds.
As it stills, she takes a tentative peck.

And that night I slept a long time, dreamed
of my son and saw him shimmering as if
through isinglass, his perch precarious
on a rough branch, listening
for my song, still waiting for my hand.

When You Were Five

You were eight when old Rainy died; we buried
him high up on the hill where pine trees sigh
and sing in the rain. *When you got married?*
that baby? did it die? you ask, *Will I*

be buried there too? And my words still clot,
then jumble out, tumbled like Scrabble tiles.
Today you are twenty and I am not
any closer to explaining things; miles

between us, miles and wings. You say, *I'm fine.*
But I recall a day when you were five.
I held your hand (then, you still wanted mine)
and that dumb dog stuck his snout in a hive

of yellow jackets. Your laces were undone.
Even then, I could only holler, *Run!*

Flight From Philly

Sometimes you're too tired
to be charitable, too irritable
to be kind, the mind bent
on whatever sleep can be plied
on a cross-country flight at night.

I'm tired you think
as you sink to your seat
in row ten, two rows up
from the toddler who when
you first glimpsed him then,
at the gate, *knew* the odds were great
you'd meet again.

At first you're amused
and wish he'd just sleep,
ditch the high-pitched diatribe
of purely pissed-off kid.
At first you feel for the haggard dad,
but that charity doesn't last
as cries crescendo. You boarded
at five-forty-five, you land at nine *your* time,
he's still in full throat at ten-to.

And all along the father placates, placates,
sings him soothing songs,
shushes and shushes

till you just want to punch him,
the timbre of these protestations
not those of pain or hunger
but anger, frustrations
this child has always
been allowed to blubber.

Then you recall how you'd detest
advice given you in false kindness
- how *you* should raise *your* boy.
And you think of your child
and your failures there.
How would it be fair to criticize?

Weren't you the one who
shamed your son for not knowing
that slob in Costco wouldn't watch
where *she* was going? Wasn't it you
who refused to understand,
who sometimes wouldn't take his hand?
And all those times you'd let him cry?

And you think of fleeing refugees,
and that mother who smothered her child
so its noises would not reveal
the place they hid. And you figure,
if *we* were, now, taking flight,

refugees heading for a homeland,
we wouldn't stand a chance.
You glance back over your shoulder,
see the hapless dad, the screwed up
face mid-cry, think, there,
but for the grace of God, go I.

Virga

(precipitation that evaporates before ever reaching the ground)

The mountains appear
both near and far,
in the painting
and a road leads
toward a ragged horizon,
just as this road
brings me here to this
uneven place. I want
to recall now
how I felt then,
when I painted it, fresh
from the arctic circle,
the Dempster,
the Top of the World.
No one.
A landscape so vast
and ancient it seemed
to never have been
inhabited by anything
but mastodon.
In the left corner, rain
that never hits the ground,
but leaves a dazzle
where it danced,
sweet and wet
as a new lover,
as tied to this land

as my hand to the brush
that made it. And I want
to go back there
to feel again
the damp hand of God
on my forehead
easing my uneasiness
with the human race,
my face moist with mist,
my fists unclenching.

Now, Since the Grass Has All Grown Back

I'm giving away the fence posts
that corralled a childhood dream
– wild sable brush of tail,
flaxen mane, surprising legs
that can carry more
than the body's own weight
but buckle far too readily.
And oh the O of nostril
flared in pain or expectation,
face all blaze and ears pricked.
Sweet smell of sweat and hay.
Wrested, rendered.
Some other girl will build
a pasture, curry a coat, breathe
the sacred scent, then miss
what she had only borrowed.

Toward September

All last night the wind
howled toward September,

answering the scream of screens
and clang of metal on mast.

It's time to leave this place.

The loons are rafting up,
eight this evening, gusting

across the surface like squalls,
feeding to fatten for their journeys

to Florida, the Carolinas,
New Orleans, where they

will cast off their costumes
of satin black and brilliant white

for brown and dusky gray. Only
those ruby jewels, their eyes, will remain

the same, constant as the constellations,
to find the way back home.

What A Horse Knows

The brain of a horse, I'm told, is about
the size of a walnut, not much

bigger than the dome of poll,
that sensitive spot behind his ears,

or his eye that can make a mountain lion
out of a stump, a silhouette, crouched

along the trail. His broom of tail will swish,
switch. Pleasure? Pain? I can't tell

this day while I curry his coat, nuzzle
his velvet muzzle as he breathes

my breath and I breathe his, and lead
him to a silent place, soft, for his knees

to buckle, sunk in the summer-
scented duff of pine needles,

where the needle finds its mark –
an iridescent neck seething

with the blood to take the drug
to his scuffled heart

and brain that has somehow
always known I mean him no harm –

but for that second.
For that second

he knows and tries
to escape the rag of his body,

to flee with the herd he never had,
that mare fat with foal, flaxen

mane flying, even as his flat eye
strikes the ground.

Nothing Can Be Returned

No one could see
the thin brown line
as it traveled from navel
to pubis, a straight-down
path, the downy hairs
aligned.

They couldn't see
the black cell swell.
Insistent.

germ cell, ovarian

You barely heard the words
under harsh lights on
a sunny afternoon
while US planes took aim
on Libyan fighters, while
the Exxon Valdez still navigated
Prince William Sound, while
thousands of Chinese students
prepared to march on
Tienamen Square.

cysplatin, vinblastine

Not fully formed,
no one could tell –
your breasts did not weep.

No one could hear
the private drum,
the rush and hush of it, the push
and pull of its tide

seaweed, dilation, extraction

while your pregnant neighbor
drowned in her vodka before
her wide-eyed slope-faced child,
while your dogs sat silent
in their kennel, waiting,
while your husband wept
without a sound.

Units of Measurement

All things grow with time, but grief
Yiddish Proverb

Nothing grows in grief, but time.

You measure growth in days
not inches marked on walls, multiply
the mass of no memories. Twenty weeks,
now twenty years. You wonder

where he'd be now
if he'd come out whole, howled
at the cold, the harshness of the light.
You can't recall the seconds passing, time
the beat of a pulse stilled. You measure loss
in fractions.

Your dogs pace their kennels, like wolves
waiting for a handout. Waiting for anything.
Live with wolves, you learn
to howl.

Your body testifies, weighs
your vacancy, calculates how long
it will take for you to disappear.

Anechoic

I've heard the absence of sound
can be louder than its presence,

blood rushes – surf in the ears –
the brain's static stippling

like floaters in your eyes. Today
I saw a man sitting on the curb,

scuffed shoes V-ed in the gutter,
knees splayed. Spidery hands

pressed tight to his ears –
mouth opening, closing, opening –

no cry. I've heard thoughts
can make noise, tip-tapping away,

quick-flapping like moths.
Like moths, absence flutters,

almost there, not there, here.
Ah, sometimes I can hear you.

The Poem as Bird

*The writing of poetry is not a craft! We are
making birds, not birdcages!* Dean Young
    – *The Art of Recklessness*

If I could build a bird, I'd start
with the eye, onyx bead,
impassive, aware.

Then I'd assemble
the wings, the things that lift
the words from the page, weightless
complication of hollow bones and feathers.

Then the breast, its tiny mighty heart
rushed and hushed,
tense and desperate.

Acknowledgements

Many thanks to these publications in which various renditions of the following poems first appeared:

Adanna Literary Journal – "I've Heard Twelve-Thousand Bees"

Autumn Sky Poetry #4 – "And This Remains"

Bellevue Literary Review – "Climacteric"

Crab Creek Review – "Units Of Measurement"

Floating Bridge Review – "Wild" and "In My Next Life I Might Be a Moth"

Flyway: Journal of Writing and Environment – "The Mountain Shrugged," "Narrow and True," "Waiting," "Winter Songs," "Gone Like Ghosts," "A Distant V," "Inside Passage – Prince William Sound"

Generations Literary Journal – "Like That"

Gertrude Press – "Passing"

Filled With Breath – 30 Sonnets by 30 Poets, Exot Books – "A Day Like Any Other" also reprinted in *Irressistable Sonnets,* Headmistress Press

Loch Raven Review – "Crossings"

Naugatuck River Review – "My Father Took Each Dying Bird"

Poetry for the Mind's Joy, Library of Congress – "Birdland"

Prime Number – "Undone"

Quiddity – "Stones in Our Pockets," "Harbor" and "Broken Water"

San Pedro River Review – "Birding at the Potholes" also
   reprinted in *Flyway* and *Raven Chronicles*
Taking Turns – *Sonnets from the Eratosphere,* Maverick Duck
   Press – "When You Were Five" also published on
   Web del Sol, IBPC
Web del Sol, IBPC – "Comfort" and "Cocooned"

Also from Cynthia Neely

Broken Water
2011 winner of the Hazel Lipa Poetry Chapbook Prize
Flyway: Journal of Writing and Environment

About the Author

Cynthia Neely lives with her husband and son up a mountain road in the Cascade foothills in North Central Washington and spends her summers on an island in Georgian Bay, Canada. These places have been indelibly etched into her persona and thus into her poetry and paintings. When she travels from these areas she invariably heads north. The natural world and her place in it have always been important to her and to her work.